D0018668

THE NON-ELECTRIC LIGHTING SERIES

BOOK 1: CANDLES

Text & Photos by Ron Brown
Cover by FK
Copyright © 2014 Ronald B. Brown
All rights reserved.
ISBN 978-0-9853337-4-4

R&C Publishing

Newark Valley, New York

ISBN 978-0-9853337-3-7

Published by
R&C Publishing
15 Dr. Knapp Road South
Newark Valley, NY 13811

Printed in the United States of America

Table of Contents

Foreword

Candles have always been a part of my life. My first memories of candles were to celebrate joyous occasions, namely birthday parties, Chanukah, and Christmas (for my Christian friends). What kid does not remember those events growing up?

Later, during my high school and college years, candles were used for a more meaningful purpose. Candlelight vigils were common during the 60s and 70s and to this day, are used to show support for various causes or to memorialize a tragedy.

With the dawn of the 21st century, mainstream awareness of the need to be prepared for disasters large and small became mainstream. In addition to the need for food, water and shelter came the need for light, because after all, who wants to be blundering around in total darkness during a power outage? This spawned a whole new industry; solar-charged and crank-up flashlights became popular as did all manner of lanterns.

Despite the popularity of these devices, many people still turn to candles for emergency lighting. They pick up tapers or votives on sale or at the dollar store as a hedge against the day the power goes out. It's more than the fact that batteries don't last forever. There's something primitive, primal, about candles. They're the comfort food of illumination.

My introduction to the more technical aspect of candles, candlelight and candle-making occurred when I read Ron Brown's book, *Lanterns, Lamps & Candles: A User's Guide*. To be honest, after reading Ron's book, I had to put aside my 60s-era concept of candle making as nothing more than a fun-but-messy hobby.

I came to realize that candles are a feasible, practical method of providing light in a grid-down situation. They've been around for a long time. And you can make them yourself — you really can — using inexpensive materials commonly available at the nearest grocery or craft store.

An epiphany? An earth-shattering revelation? Perhaps not. On the other hand, my interest in becoming a Prepper of the highest order (someone who prepares for an unexpected emergency or disaster) dictated that this was something I needed to learn to do myself, up close and personal. Making candles myself? Who would ever have thought it?

Candles is a book for the do-it-yourselfer. It is rich with photographs so even if you are not a fan of following step-by-step instructions, you will be able to construct your own candles easily and safely. Wicks, waxes, oils and containers — here in this book is everything you need to know to get started. So what are you waiting for?

Gaye Levy
February 2014

❦❧❧❦❦❧❧

Want to learn more about basic preparedness? Please visit Gaye's website at www.backdoorsurvival.com where you will find tools for creating a self-reliant lifestyle through thoughtful prepping and optimism.

So Let's Get Started

This book, *Candles*, is our first adventure in *The Non-Electric Lighting Series*. The series is aimed at people who want to survive whatever it is that Mother Nature throws at us next — blizzards, blackouts, or Carrington events.

This is a series of KISS books (Keep It Simple, Stupid). And DIY books (Do It Yourself). This volume, *Candles*, is about producing LIGHT. Not aromatherapy. Not ambiance. LIGHT.

It shows you how to make candles; how to improvise candles; how to improvise candleholders. It describes different kinds of wicks and waxes and substitutions. It gives you a leg up, a better-than-even chance of coping when a blackout finds you far from home.

But it's equally important to know what NOT to do. YouTube has several videos on emergency candles, some of which are in error and pose huge dangers. And YouTube is not alone. What part of FIRETRUCK don't you understand? This book seeks to reveal as much folly and as many hazards as possible.

We have an ancient, subconscious, primal attraction to candles. It's rooted in the human psyche. We light candles at weddings and funerals and birthdays and intimate candlelight dinners. Candles are sprinkled throughout our proverbs. Don't burn your candle at both ends. 'Tis better to light one candle than to curse the darkness.

But, embedded in our psyche or not, candles aren't for everyone.

A woman I've known for many years once admitted to me that she didn't even know how to change a light bulb until she was married . . . at age 43. She'd been raised with maids and servants. Her new husband insisted that she learn.

She laughs about it today, telling how she sat on the bed and cried until he forced her to do it.

Frankly, if you can relate to that woman's plight . . . to her angst and fears . . . if changing a light bulb pushes the limits of your mechanical expertise . . . then I question whether you or she should experiment with candles.

'Tis better to **not** light one candle than to burn the house down.

Safety
A couple of serious issues here. For one thing, lead poisoning from metal-core wicks is a hidden danger in votive candles. The tiny metal wire in the center of the wick provides support

and prevents the wick from keeling over and drowning the flame in a pool of liquid wax. U.S. manufacturers stopped using lead in 1974 but I've seen estimates that 30% of the votive candles on store shelves today still contain lead even though there are substitutes that can and should be used.

The most obvious safety issue with candles is the fact that they employ a live flame and pose a fire hazard. Fluttering window curtains are a no-no. Dangling hair smells bad when it burns. And I can tell you on very good authority that it's possible to knock over a lit candle by opening a kitchen cabinet door into it.

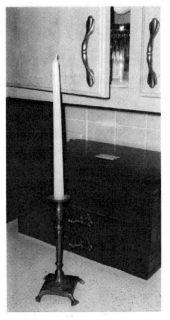

■ **ABOVE:** *What's that 911 number again? Oh yeah. I remember.* ■

The National Fire Protection Association has a variety of articles on candle safety:
http://www.nfpa.org/search.asp?query=candles

Candle Types

There is some overlap of terminology in the candle world. This section identifies how various candle types are defined within this book.

■ **ABOVE:** *Taper candles* are long, slender candles. The 10-inch candles shown here weigh 55 grams each and burn nearly eight hours. At three for a buck, that's 4.1 cents per hour. ■

A hundred years ago, the word "candle" conjured up the image of a taper. Today, "candle" translates into jar candles of the type sold by Yankee Candle at the mall outlet store. Even as we speak, on eBay, there are 48,000 pairs of candlesticks for sale. Silver, brass, and glass. They were made to hold tapers but nobody wants them anymore.

■ **ABOVE:** *Tea candles* derive their name from their use in teapot warmers. They have a variety of names and spellings: tea-lites, tcandles, etc. With a tea candle, wax is encased in a thin metal cup *or tub. This makes for an efficient use of wax. It can't drip on the table and escape. All the wax, all the fuel in the tub, is consumed. Tea candles are 1½" in diameter. High-end tea candles from Ms. Snooty's Boutique are ⅝" thick. Cheapies from the Dollar Store are ⅜" thick and burn three hours. There's also a middle size that's ½" thick.* ■

■ **ABOVE:** ***Votive candles*** *(prayer candles) are typically placed on an altar or gravesite, protected from wind and rain by some sort of candleholder. People who set out votive candles value lengthy burn times over illumination. Votives thus have small-diameter wicks and don't provide much light. The votives pictured above are 1⅜" in diameter, 2" inches high, and weigh 50 grams.* ■

■ **ABOVE:** *Jar candles* (container candles) are self-contained. The wax (usually scented) is poured directly into the jar that also holds the wick. When lit, the candle flame burns inside the container. Jar candles produce more "atmosphere" than light and often transform themselves into "cavern candles" (below). ■

■ **ABOVE:** *Pillar candles* are big enough to be freestanding and not require a candlestick. Here you can see the size difference between a pillar and a votive. This pillar is 3" in diameter, 5½" tall, and weighs 1 lb. 2 oz. Pillar candles typically become cavern candles (below). ■

MATERIALS

Wax

Whether we make our own candles or just buy them, we should know something about the materials from which they're made.

Tallow. For a zillion years, candles were made of tallow. *Tallow* is rendered fat from cows and sheep. Tallow is slow-cooked out of the meat similar to bacon grease in a frying pan. Another method is to boil the meat and skim the fat off the water afterwards. The rendering process smells terrible; back in the day, rendering plants were banned in many cities. In contrast to tallow, *lard* is rendered pig fat. Lard, like butter, is only semi-solid at room temperature. But tallow is solid, hard. The operative words are *at room temperature*.

On hot summer nights, tallow candles sag. Beef tallow melts at 109° F. Sheep tallow melts at 116° F. If you buy some authentic tallow candles, they will become a pourable liquid before the thermometer reaches 120° F. Else they are not really tallow.

The smell issue is worth elaborating for those folks whose aim it is to be self-sufficient. My mother, thrifty soul, sometimes rendered pork fat from home-butchered hogs and made her own lard with which to bake. Her homemade bread and piecrust were outstanding. But the rendering process reeked. She stunk up the house for days. I'm sure that beef and mutton tallow smell just as bad. It's just one of those real-life things that folks who talk up homesteading and self-reliance neglect to mention.

Paraffin. ($4 per lb.) Paraffin wax, made from petroleum, came along in the mid-1800's. It, too, had a low melting temperature. But with the addition of stearic acid or stearin (isolated from tallow of all things) its melting point was raised to 125-165° F (depending on grade). By the turn of the century (i.e. 1900) tallow was out and paraffin was in. In my lifetime, I've read about tallow candles but have never actually seen one.

Beeswax. ($10 per lb.) Beeswax forms the honeycomb inside a beehive. For every ten pounds of honey produced, the bees make only one pound of wax. That makes it expensive. But with a melting point of 145° F, beeswax makes excellent candles.

Soy Wax. ($5 per lb.) Soy wax is hydrogenated soybean oil. Hydrogenation (treating with hydrogen and a catalyst) is the same process that turns liquid vegetable oil into Crisco. The melting temperature of soy wax is 120-180° F, depending on the blend.

Palm Wax. ($5 per lb.) Made from the oil palm of Southeast Asia. I think of palm trees as producing coconuts. The oil palm, however, produces fruits the size of plums from which cooking oil is extracted. The liquid oil is hydrogenated to form a solid wax with a melting temperature of 140° F.

Paraffin, beeswax, soy, and palm are the only waxes you're likely to find in the candle-making aisle of your local craft store. How do they compare to each other? To answer that, I made some homemade tea candles and tested them side by

14

side . . . same wick, same tub, same amount of wax. I tested some lard and some butter while I was at it.

Test Results

Average minutes burned per 12 grams of wax:

Butter:	105 minutes
Lard:	105 minutes
Soy Wax:	105 minutes
Paraffin Wax:	115 minutes
Beeswax:	115 minutes
Scrap Candle Wax:	116 minutes
Palm Wax:	117 minutes*

* The palm wax had a 1-inch high flame whereas everything else had a 2-inch flame.

The results contradicted received wisdom. Beeswax did not burn longer than paraffin. It burned the same. Perhaps beeswax' reputation for burning longer than "regular" candles harks back a hundred years to the era when "regular" meant tallow (?).

To appease the beeswax fans, I followed up by burning a UCO paraffin "9-hour" candle in a UCO candle lantern, then a UCO beeswax candle in the same lantern. The beeswax candle weighed 62 grams at the start; the 9-hour candle, 55 grams. The 9-hour candle (so-called) lasted 12¾ hours; the beeswax candle, 14½ hours. Results-wise, the beeswax candle weighed 13% more and burned 14% longer. Sorry, beeswax fans.

In the homemade tea-candle test, I used a large-diameter wick that produced a big flame. I kept the candles trimmed to just below their smoke point throughout.

It was interesting to me that all of the candles burned with the same degree of yellowness or whiteness in their flames. I would have been hard pressed to pick out the brightest. Were these diamonds, the brilliance — the fiery sparkle — was the characteristic I sought to evaluate. To my eye they all looked the same.

Bad Info

Beeswax. Internet Quotes . . .

● "Beeswax Candles are a better option because they burn cleaner, burn much, much longer . . ."
● "Our candles are rolled from a solid sheet of beeswax and that is why they have 'ridiculously long burn times'."
● "Finally, one of the most obvious benefits of beeswax candles is that they last much longer than other forms of wax . . ."
● Tim Matson, in *The Book of Non-Electric Lighting*, 2008, states that a 12-inch beeswax candle will burn "several hours" longer than a paraffin candle of the same size.

●● *In my tea-candle test, ceteris paribus (other factors being held constant), paraffin burned for 115 minutes and beeswax burned the same, 115 minutes.*

Soy Wax. Internet Quotes . . .

● "They [soy candles] last longer than wax candles . . ."
● "[Soy wax] Burns up to 25% longer . . ."
● "Soy candles last longer — They can last up to 50% longer than paraffin candles."

●● *In my test, paraffin burned 115 minutes and soy wax burned 105 minutes.*

There's an old saying: "Paper takes ink." Meaning that paper is totally passive. You can print anything upon it you desire: truth, half-truth, falsehood. In other words, don't believe something just because you see it in print.

Let's update that. Paper takes ink but the Internet takes anything.

Wicks

Wicks bring molten wax to the candle flame by capillary action. Wicks, to perform successfully, must be a natural fiber (e.g. cotton). Synthetic materials — nylon, rayon, polyester — will not work. Synthetic fibers melt in the heat of the flame and seal off capillary action.

NOTE: It is said that many different natural fibers can be used for wicking (e.g. jute, linen, wool). And it all looks good on paper. Just remember the survivalist's adage: "If you haven't done it yourself, it doesn't work."

Flat Wicks

Candlewicks are produced by braiding or plaiting. (Braiding is done with three strands; plaiting, with more than three). Just as braids of human hair are flat rather than round like rope, a braided candlewick is flat.

Flat wicks curl as they burn . . . a good thing. The charred wick is looped back into the flame and is itself consumed, turned to ash (this is termed self-trimming). Were it not so, the exposed, on-fire section of wick would get longer and longer and the flame would get bigger and bigger. Each braided or plaited wick contains several "plies." The total number of plies in a wick determines its size. Sizes range from 15 to 60-ply.

Square Wicks

Today, square wicks are used in jar candles. But they were originally developed for beeswax. On-line candle-making forums are full of beginners' questions about beeswax. A common complaint is that beeswax votive candles stop burning about ¾ of the way down. The advice in generations past would have been to use a heavier wick.

■ ABOVE: *A taper candle made from a rolled sheet of beeswax.* ■

The numbering and sizing convention for square wicks varies by manufacturer. Why? Because if you find a wick that burns exceptionally well in the particular candles you are making, then a standard, industry-wide nomenclature would let you shop around for the same wick at a better price. But an incomprehensible, proprietary nomenclature locks you in as a client . . . or tries to. See? These shenanigans have been around longer than Microsoft. It's comforting to know that some things never change.

Cored Wicks

When burning, the wicks in jar candles and votive candles (prayer candles) must stand and burn in a pool of molten wax without buckling or falling over. That requires a tab or foot on the bottom of the wick plus a rigid core in the center. Traditional cores were lead wire. Today, cores are made of zinc, cotton, paper, and hemp.

What Size Wick to Use

Personally, I prefer a heavy wick. I want light to see by. I want as big a flame as possible. Pictured left of the pencil point is a 30-ply flat wick. Right of the pencil point is a 50-ply square wick. (Did I count the plies? Yes.) They both give a nice 2-inch high flame in homemade tea candles although the 50-ply pushes the smoke limit. Smoking is a bad habit.

Improvised Wicks

You will find many balls and skeins of string at flea markets, Dollar Stores, and tucked away in the attic. How do you know it's cotton and not synthetic? Answer. If it resists breaking and has a high tensile strength, it is likely synthetic or a synthetic blend.

Okay. It feels like cotton, smells like cotton, and tastes like cotton . . . but will it work? Answer. Try it and see. There's no other way.

Crochet thread is reputed to work well. J&P Coats brand Speed Cro-Sheen contains 8 plies. Braiding three pieces together thus yields a 24-ply wick. Don't confuse Speed Cro-Sheen with Knit Cro-Sheen or Lustersheen or bouclé (pronounced boo-CLAY). Coats & Clark brand uses a numbering system. Like candlewicking, crochet-thread terminology is an art form.

You'll often see phrases like, "100% cotton, mercerized." The important part is 100% cotton. "Mercerized" means the thread was soaked in caustic soda while under tension; the end product is more lustrous as a result. Mercer was the guy who invented the process.

Mordants

Mordants are used in textiles to set the dye so the color doesn't run whereas mordents (note the spelling difference) are used in musical notation.

I've seen three reasons listed as the purpose of soaking candlewicks in a mordant — to make the flame brighter; to make the wick burn more slowly (so its burn rate is equal to the melt rate of the wax); and to cause the wick to curl (so as to be self-trimming).

The part about making the flame brighter caught my eye so I tried the three most commonly cited mordants: (1) turpentine, (2) vinegar, and (3) a solution of boric acid, salt, and water. There are others.

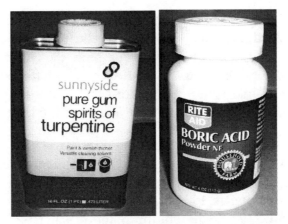

■ **ABOVE:** *You'll find turpentine with the paint thinners at the hardware store and boric acid with first aid supplies in the drugstore. It's used as an eyewash.* ■

So will a mordant give you a brighter candle flame?

I soaked a variety of wicks in a variety of mordants, numbered everything, dried them, prepped them, tabbed them, made some tubs, melted some wax, poured some tea candles, and spent a couple of hours observing them burn. It didn't cost much. Just an evening of my life.

Brilliancy-wise there was no difference in the flames. They were interchangeable.

As regards length of burn, the results were — to use proper statistical jargon — confounded. In fact, in the case of 30-ply flat wicks, "untreated" burned longer than anything else.

How best to summarize my findings? Well, let's just say I'll cut you a deal on some boric acid.

MAKING CANDLES

Melting Wax

Once upon a time, some enterprising teenage friends of my wife decided to make candles. So the wax went into the saucepan and the saucepan went onto the stove and ten minutes later they had an on-fire, blazing, flaming pot of wax. Panic time. They didn't burn the house down but one girl ended up in the doctor's office with severe leg burns.

DO NOT melt wax in a pan setting directly on a stove burner. The books say that at only 395° F paraffin wax can explode and splatter flaming wax in all directions: without warning; without smoking or bubbling beforehand. Candle wax melts well below 212° F (the boiling point of water) so there's no need to get it any hotter than that.

The Digiorno pizza box says to preheat the oven to 400° F. That means, were you to put a pan of candle wax in the oven, it would explode spontaneously, all by itself, just about the time you were ready put in the pizza. Once more with feeling, what part of ⚡**FIRE**⚡ don't you understand?

The traditional way to safely melt wax was in a double boiler (described below). Today, there are alternatives.

Can you use a crock-pot? Many people do.

As a test, I melted some old candles in a crock-pot. With the setting on high, the temperature reached 275° F at the two-hour mark. Half an hour later it was 315° and still climbing. The perfume smell had been replaced by a scorched smell. Stirring with a wooden spoon resulted in much crackling and bubbling. I chickened out. I switched the setting to low. An hour later the temperature had dropped and stabilized at 200° F.

Can you use the microwave? Many people do.

■ **ABOVE:** *The instructions for the Microwaveable Soy Wax shown here say, "Place soy wax into microwave safe container . . . and place in microwave. Depending on how powerful your microwave is, melt wax from 30 seconds to 1 minute. Check wax. If the wax is completely melted check temperature to see if it is ready. Microwave longer as needed until wax temperature is 180° F. NEVER LEAVE THERMOMETER IN WAX WHEN PLACING IT IN MICROWAVE! . . . Do not exceed 300° F when melting soy wax.*

Wax may catch fire." [Please note that "microwaveable" soy wax can also be melted in a double boiler.] ■

I must confess to misgivings about microwaving. What happens to food if you accidentally enter 15 minutes instead of 15 seconds? Or let's say the kids see you melt wax in the microwave and later decide to make some candles on their own while you're gone for the afternoon? OF COURSE they'll read the directions first.

Can you use an electric coffee-mug warmer to melt wax? I've seen it recommended on YouTube.

■ **ABOVE:** *The Mr. Coffee mug warmer shown here draws 17 watts of electricity. It took 1½ hours to melt 2½ ounces of wax. At that point, with the wax just barely melted, the wax temperature was 140° F. After setting undisturbed on the warmer for another hour, the wax temperature reached 160° F. The cubes of wax seen on the right side of the picture are from scrap candles melted down at an earlier time and poured into an ice cube tray.* ■

So, is a coffee-mug warmer safe? Well, it's slow, I can assure you of that. The better question is: Does the method at hand pose an acceptable level of risk? And the answer is: Only you can decide.

Of course, in a SHTF scenario (i.e. fecal matter hits the fan), you won't have a choice. Devices that require electricity (crock-pots, microwaves, and coffee-mug warmers) won't be operational. You'll be limited to the double-boiler method.

Double Boiler

Personally, the only way I melt candle wax is in a double boiler. I don't even need a thermometer; the wax temperature cannot go above the boiling point of water.

■ **ABOVE:** *A double boiler. The large pan setting on the burner holds water; the smaller pan nests into the larger pan and never gets hotter than 212° F, the boiling point of water.* ■

■ **ABOVE:** *An improvised double boiler. It works well. Candle making is good, clean, messy fun IF you use a double boiler.* ■

• How to Make Taper Candles

Candles (that is, tapers) are easily made by hand dipping. There is no law that says candles must be dipped in multiples. In the interest of simplicity they can be dipped one-at-a-time. They burn just fine.

■ **ABOVE:** *Nut tied in end of wicking to keep the wick straight when dipping. It can be cut off after a few dips.* ■

■ **ABOVE:** *The wick's other end is tied to a wrench that serves as dipping handle and drying counterweight.* ■

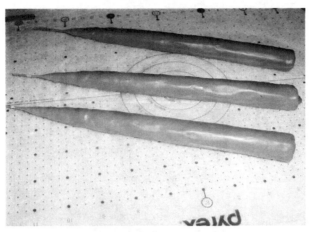

■ **ABOVE:** *Finished candles. Hand-roll them across a flat, hard surface while they are still warm.* ■

■ **ABOVE LEFT:** *Many people use a glass vase as a dipping cylinder or vat. I recommend against it. Glass does not transfer heat well. If the wax hardens in the cylinder, it takes f-o-r-e-v-e-r to get it melted again.* **ABOVE RIGHT:** *I cut/overlapped/soldered two tin cans together to make a dipping vat. I am not especially good at soldering. Finally resorted to epoxy glue to get the last little leak stopped. But then it worked fine.* ■

■ **ABOVE:** *From the bottom up — stove burner, saucepan with boiling water, dipping vat filled with molten wax, wooden dowel for stirring rod. The aluminum pie pan serves as a cover to keep the heat focused where you want it. Else the water boils away and you use a truly excessive amount of fuel.* ■

Procedure

1. Fill the dipping vat with molten wax. Keep the vat in a saucepan of boiling water for the duration. Use a heat shield (see the cutout pie pan above) to keep the heat close to the vat.

2. While waiting for the wax to melt, cut the wicks to length, tie a weight to the bottom of each wick so that it will hang straight, and tie the top of each wick to a heavy handle. I used box-end wrenches (see above photos).

3. Make sure in advance you have sufficient counter space to hang all the candles you are making (a dozen at a setting is about the right amount with this rig). Dip the candles in order. By the time you finish the twelfth, the first is cool enough to dip again.

4. To dip, pick up the handle (wrench) and lower the dangling wick into the vat. On the very first dip, hold the wick in the bath a few seconds so that the wick soaks up some wax. After that, each dip is a quick in-and-out. Don't linger. You don't want the molten wax in the vat to re-melt what has already been deposited on the candle.

5. After a dozen dips or so, the candle is heavy enough to hang vertically on its own and you can cut off the initial weight (nut) you started with.

6. Add wax to the vat as needed. You'll be consuming it as you go.

7. After 35-40 dips, the butt end of the candle will be ¾" in diameter and the dipping is over.

8. Empty the vat. Don't let the wax harden in it.

9. Roll the warm candles on a flat, hard surface (like a child rolling out a worm of clay). It straightens them.

10. In fact, that's a good way to straighten bent candles in general. Soak them in a pan of warm water. When they are warm to the touch, roll them out on a flat, hard surface.

Yard sales and Goodwill Stores are a great source of wax. Soiled Christmas candles, bent tapers, and half-burned pillars can be had for pennies on the dollar. More than once (after Y2K) I bought a shoebox full of candles for a quarter. At times, when someone was packing up at the end of a yard sale, I've been given a handful of candles for free.

• How to Make Tea Candles

The advantage of tea candles is that the wax can't melt and drip away and escape the flame as it can with tapers. The container holds the molten wax in place. All of it gets fed to the flame. For the time you spend and the results you get, tea candles are a better bet than tapers.

I say this in the context of obtaining light — illumination — not pretty decorations.

Improvised Tabbed Wicks

■ **ABOVE:** *Every time that happened, the glass broke (due to unequal expansion of the glass; hot on one side and cold on the other). As opposed to this, a tea candle is short enough that the wick only needs to be tabbed (i.e. footed) to prevent falling. A support wire or core inside the stubby little wick is not necessary.* ■

And so, to start making tea candles, we need wicks — tabbed wicks, wicks with feet, wicks that can stand upright on their own. In *Lanterns, Lamps & Candles* I gave somewhat lengthy directions on how to make metal tabs. But I've found an easier way. We're going to use a sandwich of duct tape and small pieces of manila-folder material rather than metal.

Even before that, however, the cotton wick material must be prepped (prepared). The prepping consists of soaking the wicks in molten wax and then allowing them to harden.

■ **ABOVE:** *Sauté cotton string in molten candlewax. **Do not** put the pan directly on the burner. Although you can't see it from this angle, there is a saucepan of boiling water under the frying pan pictured here.* ■

■ **ABOVE:** *There are other ways to prep a wick. We could seesaw it over a bar of paraffin wax as shown above. Or soak it in some cooking oil. Or rub lard or butter into it. But these methods all produce soft, limpy wicks. And our tea-candle wick needs to be stiff and strong so we can force it through a slightly undersize hole in a tab. The sauté-in-candle-wax method produces just what we need, a hard, rigid wick.* ■

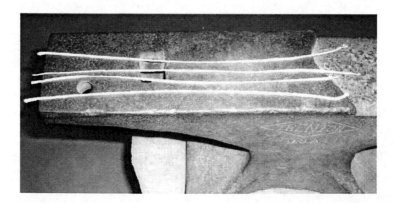

■ **ABOVE:** *Drape the sautéed wicks over an anvil to cool and harden. It makes a great heat sink. You do have an anvil, yes?* ■

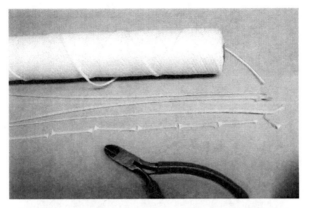

■ **ABOVE:** *Cut the prepped wick into 1" lengths.* ■

■ **ABOVE:** *At "noon" we see the corner of a manila folder. At 1:00 PM there is a roll of duct tape. At 3:00 PM, dime-sized squares of manila-folder material. At 4:00 PM, squares of folder material stuck to pieces of duct tape. At 6:00 PM the duct tape is folded over the manila folder material, making a sandwich. At 7:00 PM are*

scissors. At 10:00 PM are sandwiches-cum-tabs that have been trimmed. At 11:00 PM we see tabs with their sharp corners clipped off. ∎

∎ **ABOVE:** *Next we must get a hole through the tab. A scratch awl works. A darning needle works. How big a hole? It's impossible to give a number because the wick you use will be different from what I use. Some experimentation is required. You have to be able to thread the prepped wick through the hole (barely) and then slide the tab (with some degree of force) to the other end of the wick. It's not really difficult or overly complicated; it's easier than tying your shoes.* ∎

■ **ABOVE:** *Cutting the wick schmushed out the end of the wick. Good. That stops it from falling through the hole in the tab.* ■

■ **ABOVE:** *Push the cold-and-hard wick through the hole. Push the tab down to the bottom of the wick. Crimp the tab around the wick as best you can with your fingers and fingernails. And that's it; you're done. Wicks tabbed in this fashion are surprisingly robust. Although other materials work (pasteboard tablet backs and Scotch tape, for example) of all the things I've tried, manila folders and duct tape beat the competition by a country mile.* ■

Improvised Tubs

■ **ABOVE:** *The aluminum tubs used for commercial tea candles can be reused but are easily damaged. Inspect each one (to detect leakers) before making a mess with molten wax. Trust me.* ■

■ **ABOVE:** *Here I tried a bent pin for a tab and a plastic bottle cap for a tub. At the end of the burn, the flame melted a hole in the plastic. Oops.* ■

Metal bottle caps (vitamins, catsup, olive oil) work well as tubs but are gradually being replaced by plastic. Plastic does not work. At the end of the burn, the candle flame will melt a hole through the bottom of a plastic bottle cap.

Fortunately, metal tubs are easy to make from aluminum foil. Below, a mini-muffin tin serves as the female die and a shot glass as the male. It's a marriage made in heaven.

■ **ABOVE:** *First, a 4" x 4" square of foil is pressed between the dies. Next, the foil is roughly trimmed so that no ears stick up for a spoon of molten wax to bump into. The molten wax is then spooned in and a tabbed wick inserted. The only thing that remains is for the candle to cool and harden.* ■

■ **ABOVE:** *Aluminum-foil baking cups are available for mini-muffin pans but ordinary aluminum foil is easier to work with. The pre-made baking cups are springy and resist lying flat in the mold.* ■

■ **ABOVE:** *Trim the excess foil with scissors. This homemade tea candle (with its big flame) will burn for two hours.* ■

■ **ABOVE:** *What's not to like?* ■

• How to Make Jar Candles

Glass canning jars (Mason jars) were invented in 1858. But when I was a child (in the World War II era), jar candles were unknown. Why?

Today, in shopping malls, whole stores are devoted exclusively to jar candles (even though, with electric lighting, we don't really need candles of any kind). But despite today's popularity, I can remember when jar candles didn't exist. Why didn't they?

The problem, in days of yore, was that no practical method existed for attaching the candlewick to the bottom of a glass container. The world had to wait for hot glue and glue guns before jar candles became viable.

And that happened about 1965. In that year, *Popular Science* ran an article on a brand new item: hot-melt glue. And in 1969 (according to Wikipedia) Yankee Candle was born.

There are many Web sites and YouTube videos showing how to make jar candles.

You need a jar (a glass pint canning jar is ideal). You need some wax (soy wax is popular). Plus a wick that is both tabbed and cored (so it doesn't collapse and let the flame drown in the soup). Plus a way to fasten the foot of the wick to the floor of the jar. That's where the glue gun comes in.

After wasting an afternoon playing with several glues I had on hand (contact cement, super glue, model airplane cement, and epoxy to name just a few), Google revealed to me that hot-melt glue was the secret of success. And so it was.

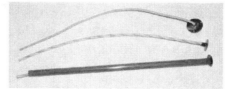

■ **ABOVE:** *Wicks come in a wide variety of flavors. Here we see (on top) a Country Lane brand wick (sold by A.C.Moore) described as a Waxed Wick, Large Paper, Item #30063. In the center is an ArtMinds brand wick (sold by Michaels). At the bottom is a footed wick inside a drinking straw. The straw serves as a jig to guide the wick when it is being positioned/glued in the jar.* ■

■ **ABOVE:** *Hot glue is applied to the foot of the wick, after which the wick (held by the straw) is bonded to the floor of the jar.* ■

■ **ABOVE LEFT:** *Here we see the wick (far left) positioned with a drinking straw for gluing. Once the foot of the wick is glued fast, the straw is withdrawn. Just to the right of that is a finished candle after the wax been poured and has hardened. The wick has been*

trimmed to ¼" above the surface of the wax. **ABOVE RIGHT:** *After the wax is poured, a jar lid with a hole punched in its center serves to keep the wick centered in the candle. Slight tension is pulled on the wick and a clothespin serves to keep the wick vertical inside the candle. (For illustrative purposes, the pieces are shown here with no wax having been poured.)* ■

■ **ABOVE:** *A jar candle made with soy wax and a "Soy Wick" (designed specifically for soy wax) branded ArtMinds. These wicks come in medium, large, and extra-large sizes. This wick is a "large" size, perfect for this wax-and-jar combo. The wick is big enough to keep the wax melted back to the walls of the jar (thus avoiding the cavern-candle syndrome) but small enough not to smoke.* ■

I must confess the failure of epoxy glue to work in a jar candle surprised me. When I glued a wick to the floor of a jar using epoxy, the bond was strong enough that I could pick the jar up by the wick. As soon as I poured in hot wax, however, the slightest tension on the wick (to straighten it) broke the bond and pulled the wick free.

One adhesive that can be used in place of hot-glue is 3M Super Weatherstrip and Gasket Adhesive. (Hat tip to GUNRNR7271 on YouTube for this one.) This adhesive is made for automobiles, not household use. I bought some on-line after not being able to find it in hardware stores. At the time, I didn't know enough to ask for it in auto supply stores.

You'll likely have to experiment to find the technique that works for you. The 3M directions say, "Apply a thin, uniform coat of adhesive on each surface but do not close bond [i.e. don't close the door; don't join the surfaces together just yet]. Allow adhesive to dry until tacky . . . [then] Assemble materials with sufficient pressure to ensure contact."

My technique is to [1] put a small gob of glue on the foot of the wick, [2] position the foot of the wick on the floor of the jar (using a straw), [3] remove the wick (thereby leaving a smear of adhesive on the floor of the jar so that both surfaces are coated with glue), [4] let everything dry for 3 minutes (to get tacky), [5] reposition the wick in the jar using a straw, [6] hold the wick in position for 10 seconds under pressure, [7] withdraw the straw and let the jar set for 20 minutes before pouring any wax. It works.

When all is said and done, I must admit that I'm not a huge fan of jar candles; they are not something you can improvise.

The wax and wick must be matched. Too small a wick makes a cavern candle. Too big a wick makes smoke.

41

The wicks cannot be homemade. Wicks must be cored as well as footed. That translates into factory-made.

Glue is the Achilles' heel of jar candles. Hot glue (a thermoplastic adhesive) works best. 3M Super Weatherstrip and Gasket Adhesive also works. But the choices stop there. There's no substitute to be found rattling around in old boxes out in the workshop.

Jar candles are not cost effective. Store-bought tea candles cost 1.7 cents per hour to run. Store-bought tapers cost 4.1 cents per hour.

Jar candles, if you make them yourself to save money, have a run rate of 5.4 cents per hour (just for the materials). That's based on the lowest (2014) Internet prices I could find. If you buy wax and wicks at brick-and-mortar craft stores like Michaels or A.C.Moore, that 5.4-cent figure triples or quadruples.

CANDLESTICKS, ETC.

Commercial Lanterns for Tapers

COLEMAN & UCO CANDLE LANTERNS. Neither am I a big fan of UCO and/or Coleman spring-loaded candle-lanterns. I own both brands. (UCO is what I used, earlier, to compare beeswax and paraffin.) These lanterns require a bastard-size candle, 1⅛" in diameter, costing about one dollar per. You can roll a larger candle over a hot surface, melt off some of its diameter, and make it fit. But, in use, the flame is too big. It doesn't work. Of course, neither UCO nor Coleman wants it to work. They want you to buy the special size.

You can't reach in to trim the wick on a candle-lantern so the flame is engineered (via wax blend and wick size) to stay small. Small flame means inferior light.

■ ABOVE: *A Coleman candle lantern on the left; a UCO candle lantern on the right; and a 1⅛" diameter candle that will fit either.* ■

Spring-loaded candle-lanterns leak wax internally, gumming up the works. Once the wax hardens, they are a beast to disassemble and reload with a new candle. On the plus side, they do resist wind and are fairly safe as regards tipping, fire hazard, etc. Fun toy for the kids. Nothing to shave by.

HURRI-CANDLES. Hurri-Candles, to use their commercial name (a play on the words "hurricane" and "candles"), seek to shelter a candle flame with a glass chimney. They work fairly well. Below is the commercial version.

Hurri-Candles tend to flutter. It seems like the flame consumes the available oxygen and dies down . . . letting in a flood of new oxygen that blows the flame around . . . then the new oxygen causes the flame to flare up . . . repeat, repeat . . .

■ **ABOVE:** **Left.** A *store-bought Hurri-Candle. Nice on the porch where it's breezy.* **Right.** *The Hurri-Candle box.* ■

Improvised Lanterns for Tapers

HOMEMADE HURRI-CANDLES. The glass chimney from a kerosene lamp and some wood scraps make a respectable "hurri-candle." They do suffer a height limitation. The kerosene chimneys are only 8½" tall whereas the commercial Hurri-Candle is 12" tall.

■ **ABOVE LEFT:** *Simple wooden cleats hold a kerosene lamp chimney (8½" tall) snugly in place. A ¾" hole in the plywood base holds the candle.* **ABOVE RIGHT:** *Who said the chimney had to be right side up? The beaded top of this particular chimney snaps perfectly into a canning jar ring. The ring is tacked to a board. A ¾" hole in the board holds the candle. ■*

■ **ABOVE:** *This picture is from the Philippines. The high wooden frame really resists wind. Torres appears to be a brand name etched in the glass. ■*

CANDLE FLASHLIGHT. The next idea came from a booklet entitled *Light* by Dawn Russell. She calls it a candle "flashlight." Hat tip to Dawn.

You'll need:

(1) A taper candle.

(2) A 3-pound coffee can (well . . . today it's 2½ lbs.) And make it a metal can, if you please, not plastic and not cardboard sprayed with a shiny metallic coating.

(3) A wire coat hanger (for a handle).

We'll operate the flashlight with the can on its side, not eye-to-the-sky. What served as the can's bottom when it held coffee becomes the back wall of the flashlight.

In use, the candle is vertical and the can is horizontal. The top of the candle sticks up through (what has become) the floor of the flashlight. The flame is at the top of the candle and inside the can. The candle's bottom end protrudes down through the floor and hangs under the flashlight. Thus you can't set the flashlight down; it must be carried or hung on a peg.

■ **ABOVE:** *The candle flashlight. To the basic design I added a round mirror on the back wall (held in place with a wire that goes crossways) plus a serrated handle (so that the flashlight can be angled up or down when hung).* ■

To build the flashlight, first remove the top of the coffee can (and the coffee, too, may I add). Then cut an X in the can wall, midway between the two ends. Each arm of the X should be an inch long. Push a candle partway through the X and into the can. The points of the X become spurs that grip the candle.

To cut the X, first punch a hole through the can wall with a nail and hammer. Then cut the metal with a utility knife. (Cans aren't very thick these days.) Use a sawing motion. Some strength is required.

A piece of wire coat hanger forms the handle. Punch two holes in the top of the flashlight (i.e. the roof over the flame). One of the holes is at the rear of the light; the other at the front.

Push the wire into one of the holes (from the outside) and, with pliers, crimp the end of the wire inside the flashlight to form a foot that will not pull back through the hole. Bend the wire as necessary and repeat the process on the second hole.

A 2½ lb. coffee can is 6" in diameter. Allow 3" of headspace between the top of the candle and the flashlight's ceiling.

Commercial Lanterns for Tea Candles

■ **ABOVE LEFT:** *Lanterns for tea candles come in all shapes and sizes. This one does shield the flame from wind and rain (which is what lanterns are for) but is useless when it comes to producing light. Then again, it wasn't made for light. It was made for decoration.* **ABOVE RIGHT:** *This lantern, because it has clear glass, appears very utilitarian and practical. The globe, however, is unique and all but impossible to duplicate or replace. If it ever breaks (and this one did), you might as well throw it out.* ■

■ **ABOVE:** *This lantern is the most practical of the three shown. The globe is clear glass, allowing all possible light to escape, and it consists of simple pieces of flat glass, easily replaced if broken. The glass panes are gripped by uncomplicated grooves or channels. If desired, you could substitute a mirror for one of the glass panes.* ■

Improvised Lanterns for Tea Candles

Not being able to set Ms. Russell's "candle flashlight" down (because the taper candle protrudes out the bottom) proved to be a pain so I worked out a couple of alternate designs (pictured below) that use tea candles and allow for set-down.

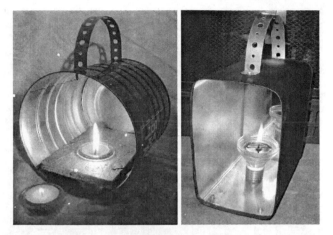

■ **ABOVE LEFT:** *I put two decking screws in the front bottom of the can to serve as feet. The rear end of the flashlight body serves as the third foot for set-down. A piece of aspenite (a.k.a. chipboard, waferboard) serves as a floor. It's held in place with screws. I drilled a 1¾" hole in the aspenite … into which I inserted a glass holder … into which I inserted a tea candle. The glass holder could be glued to the aspenite instead of setting in a drilled hole. The candle inside the flashlight with the big flame is a homemade tea candle. The candle outside the flashlight with the small flame is a store-bought tea candle.* **ABOVE RIGHT:** *Here I've used a square paint-thinner can, shortened from 9½" down to 6½". (THINK SAFETY!* **In sheet metal work, turn raw metal edges and pinch them together!)** *Inside the can, I fastened an Edison-type light-bulb socket to the floor using tiny bolts.* ■

■ **ABOVE:** *Here I superglued a condiment/prep bowl (such as TV chefs use) to the top of an electrical fuse. The Edison socket (already mounted inside the flashlight light) grips the fuse on the bottom. Above that, the prep bowl holds the tea candle.* ■

■ **ABOVE:** *It works well.* ■

■ **ABOVE:** *Another idea. A small Pyrex measuring cup makes a decent tea-candle lantern. Shown here is a one-cup size. It shields the flame from wind (good while walking) though not from rain.* ■

■ **ABOVE:** *Votive candles can also be made to work in a measuring-cup lantern. Put the candle inside a clear holder and the holder inside the cup.* ■

■ **ABOVE:** *It, too, works well.* ■

■ **ABOVE:** *Yet one more idea, an improvised reflector made from a beer can. The only tool you need is a sharp knife. Hat tip to IntenseAngler on YouTube for this one. The can's bottom is domed (meaning a tea candle won't set on it) so I turned the can upside down and removed the tab to make the base flat. A tea candle then snuggles in there quite nicely.* ■

■ **ABOVE:** *At its simplest, a tea candle will burn setting on a saucer.* ■

■ **ABOVE:** *Better than a saucer, however, is an empty baby food jar. It will protect the flame from stray breezes. The jar will slowly become too hot to pick up and move barehanded, hence the twisted wire handle.* **Caution:** *The bottom of the jar gets hot, too, not just the sides.* ■

■ **ABOVE:** *Did I mention that the bottom of the jar gets hot, too, not just the sides?* ■

If you are buying candles (rather than making them), this is the most cost-effective arrangement in the book. Tea candles are 20 for $1 in a Dollar Store. Each candle will burn three hours. That's 1.7 cents per hour. You will be hard pressed to find any candle with a lower hourly cost. The wick is small, you say? And, as a consequence, the flame is small? Then light two.

■ **ABOVE:** *It's important to keep the tea candle centered in the jar. Baby food jars are not Pyrex. If one side of the jar gets hot while the other side remains cool, the jar can crack from uneven expansion of the glass. A simple loop of Scotch tape will keep the aluminum tub centered in the jar.* ■

■ **ABOVE:** *Let's pair up [1] a tea candle in a baby food jar (with a wire handle) with [2] the improvised beer-can reflector. You can station some reflectors in the bathroom, bedroom night stand, etc., then carry the lit tea candle with you on your journey through the house and park it in a reflector as needed. To reduce smoking when you blow out the flame, place the baby food lid on the baby food jar.* ■

■ **ABOVE:** *As a variation, you can add a handle to the beer-can reflector instead of a handle on the glass jar. A mirror as a set-down station doesn't hurt anything either.* ■

THE GOOD, THE BAD AND THE UGLY

Crayon Candles

An Internet search for "emergency candles" reveals a surprising array of ideas. But not all are practical or even safe. So, in no particular order, let's review the good, the bad and the ugly. Many of these ideas (not all) come from YouTube. We'll start with crayon candles.

A UK-based survivalist, Dave Hax, presents five ways to make emergency candles. Actually, only two of the five ideas are candles: (1) crayon candles and (2) Gouda-cheese-wax candles. The other three are improvised vegetable-oil lamps and will be considered in the next book of this series (*Book 2: Vegetable-Oil Lamps*).

For crayon candles, Mr. Hax provides two variations.

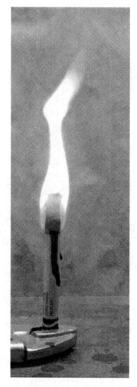

■ **ABOVE:** *Variation #1. Single crayon. The paper wrapper serves as the wick. It only required one wooden kitchen match to get this thing started. I used a pair of visegrips as a candlestick. It did burn for 30 minutes as claimed, but I'm not sure I want it in the middle of my kitchen table. A blackout is one thing; a house fire, quite another.* ■

■ **ABOVE LEFT:** *Variation #2. Three crayons wired together with a wick in the center. The wick used here was proper candle wicking and not a random piece of string. Based (presumably) on the fact that one crayon burns for half an hour, Mr. Hax projects that three crayons will burn an hour and a half. This arrangement, however, burned only 15 minutes even though the flame was tiny. Note that I removed the paper wrapping from the crayons whereas Mr. Hax does not.* **ABOVE RIGHT:** *This is the three-crayon variation, with the paper wrapping left intact, a mere two minutes into the burn. The flame is not tiny; it is life-threatening.* ■

■ **ABOVE:** *I tried crayon wax in a tea candle using the same wick that with paraffin produces a 2-inch high flame. The flame was small and the candle only burned five minutes before sputtering out. Crayons make lousy candle wax.* ■

ChapStick Candles

Several YouTube videos show how to make emergency candles from lip balm (e.g. ChapStick). But they're not safe, sorry.

■ **ABOVE LEFT:** *The YouTube videos typically show a Q-Tip (broken in half) used as a wick. The broken-stick end of the swab is stuck far down in the ChapStick tube while the cotton-fluff end does the wicking. In such an arrangement, the flame is very big and smokes badly. So I tried a prepped candlewick, trimmed to a mere ⅛" above the wax. The flame was small. Even so, within one minute the plastic ChapStick tube began to melt and sag as shown here.* **ABOVE CENTER:** *Small wick or no, after two minutes the flame was huge and the plastic tube began to melt all the way around, not just on one side.* **ABOVE RIGHT:** *Oh my stars and garters! The plastic tube wasn't melting. It was BURNING! The plastic itself was on fire. YOU might want this as a candle but Grandma and I will pass, thank you.* ■

IMCO Lighters

There's an English chap on eBay selling IMCO cigarette lighters. Developed in the 1930's, they're made in Austria and appear to be Europe's answer to the Zippo.

■ **ABOVE.** *From the eBay sales pitch: "These lighters are a great piece of kit, they are more user friendly than a Zippo, cheaper and double up as a candle . . . Runs on Lighter fluid or Petrol . . . IMCO has produced and sold over HALF A BILLION (yes half a billion!!) lighters . . ."* ■

Too bad someone might believe that "These lighters . . . double up as a candle."

■ **ABOVE:** *The set-up. I inserted the IMCO "candle" in a ⅝" diameter hole so it wouldn't get knocked over.* ■

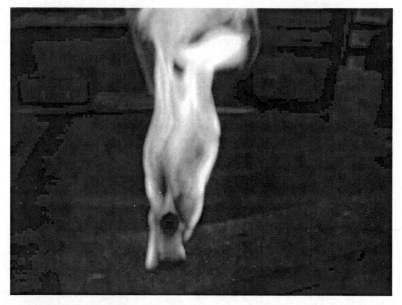

■ **ABOVE:** *This happened suddenly at 15 minutes. Sorry the focus is poor; it caught me off guard.* ■

Crisco Candles

YouTube contains several variations on the Crisco-Candle theme. In some, wicks of one sort or another are pressed directly into a can of Crisco. In others, the Crisco is spooned from the metal can into another container, typically a glass pint canning jar.

On a scale of one to ten, these things don't work. Let me first explain why they don't work and then give you a DIY KISS "candle" that does work. In case you've forgotten, that's a Do-It-Yourself-Keep-It-Simple-Stupid candle.

Technically, a Crisco Candle is not a candle. It falls more into the "vegetable-oil lamp" category. Probably you don't care about that. You just want some light.

Fair enough. But to get something that burns Crisco, I'll have to confiscate a design from *Vegetable-Oil Lamps* (Book 2 of this series). There are 12 other lamp designs in Book 2, so I'm not exactly giving away the farm.

One of the Crisco Candle designs on YouTube bills itself as a 100-hour candle. That's suspect on the face of it. The hand-dipped taper we made at the beginning of this booklet weighed 53 grams, and burned 7 hours. The so-called 100-hour Crisco Candle, based on the weight of the fuel to be burned, would likely have a burn time of 50 hours, not 100.

At its heart, Crisco is vegetable oil. It is turned into a solid by a process called hydrogenation. Hydrogen gas is bubbled through the oil in the presence of a catalyst (platinum or nickel) and the oil becomes semi-solid with a higher melting temperature than had the parent oil. You can melt Crisco, then let it cool and reharden, but it remains, in whatever form, vegetable oil.

An olive-oil lamp or a vegetable-oil lamp (and that includes Crisco) needs a fluffy wick. The strand from a cotton floor mop, a string-mop, works great. A (comparatively) tightly woven wick from a kerosene lamp doesn't work well with vegetable oil. Candle wicking works almost not at all.

■ **ABOVE:** *The so-called 100-hour Crisco Candle uses a pint canning jar with a conventional candle in its center (which, conveniently, supplies a ready-made wick). Crisco, serving as supplemental fuel, is packed between the candle and the walls of the jar.* ■

■ **ABOVE:** *The observed results are these: (1) The Crisco does not melt all the way out to the walls of the jar so it becomes a glowing "cavern candle" with a half-inch sidewall of Crisco all 'round. (2) A candlewick is not up to the task of feeding viscous vegetable oil to the flame. As a consequence, the flame is very small. In my trial, after 18 hours, it simply died. No doubt other candles would produce different results.* ■

■ **ABOVE:** *Alternate Crisco Candle designs use bigger wicks (whether improvised or factory-made) and sometimes twisted paper wicks, homemade, simply poked into the Crisco. These designs fail because the flame is too big and smokes. And I mean* **SMOKES!** *It's not something you'd want inside your house.* ■

The balance between too small a flame (producing a pinhead of light) and too big a flame (producing lots of smoke) can be resolved with a simple vegetable-oil lamp. And the one presented below is indeed simple. It's an empty tuna fish can with a hole poked in its side.

A Simple Vegetable-Oil Lamp

■ **ABOVE:** *The font (the part that holds the fuel) is simply a tuna fish can. The first order of business is to get a hole (up near the rim) through the sidewall of the can. That's where the wick will go, through the hole. A nail, a scratch awl, or a center punch will all serve to make the hole. With some love-taps from a hammer, of course.* ■

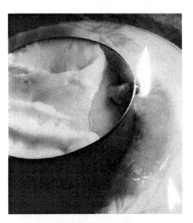

■ **ABOVE:** *The wick is a strand from a cotton string-mop. And it must be cotton; synthetics melt. The fuel is Crisco. Only the Crisco near the flame stays liquid. Every hour or so you must push a little*

63

*fuel towards the flame. The tuna can sets on a saucer to catch
drips. This is not the greatest lamp in the world but it is certainly
more practical and functional than any Crisco Candle I've seen on
YouTube. It actually works. Rudimentary lamps of this sort were
what poor people lived with, day-in-and-day-out, before Edison's
light bulb. ∎*

It should go without saying so I'll say it. The wick needs to
be prepped before you light it. "Prepping" means you
saturate the wick in oil or grease before lighting. A dry wick
poking out of a lump of Crisco won't get you very far.

Crude as it is, this lamp will burn a variety of fuels, not just
vegetable shortening or Crisco. It will burn olive oil. It will
burn other cooking oils, new, used, or rancid. It will burn
mineral oil (i.e. laxative). It will burn baby oil. It will burn
butter and lard and Vaseline and margarine. Bacon grease
will burn but it will sputter. Bacon has water injected into the
meat during the curing process. A tiny bit of water remains in
the bacon grease. It's the water that causes the sputtering.

Tip. Vegetable oil can be fiendishly difficult to light. One or
two drops of charcoal lighter fluid on the wick works
wonders.

Caution. Just because this lamp will burn many different
fuels and produce light from them does not mean that all
these different fuels smell good when they burn.

Warning. This lamp is an open-faced lamp with an open
flame. The flame is a mere whisker away from the fuel. It
will safely burn heavy, viscous oils with a high flash point
(e.g. olive oil) or semi-solid fats (butter, lard). But it is not
safe with most combustible (much less flammable) petroleum
products.

Would you purposely ignite a saucer of gasoline in the
middle of your kitchen? Well, gasoline is no more safe in a

tuna can than it is a saucer. Ditto for kerosene, Coleman fuel, and diesel fuel. Whether we call it a lamp or a tuna can, "it is what it is."

Sorry if that sounds like Alan Watts and Zen Buddhism circa 1960 but please consider the "Duncker candle problem."

A WWII-era psychologist, Karl Duncker, posed a problem in which the subject was given a candle, some matches, and a box of thumbtacks. The subject was told to mount the candle on the wall so that, when burning, it wouldn't drip on the table.

Most people tried to mount the candle on the wall using thumbtacks. They were both unsuccessful and frustrated. A small minority mounted the thumbtack BOX on the wall (using thumbtacks) and then mounted the candle on the box.

"It's a thumbtack box, dammit. Not a candlestick." That was the typical reaction of the typical subject. And that blind spot is called "functional fixedness."

Hopefully you can see how this relates to tuna fish cans-cum-vegetable oil lamps. They are both just pieces of metal, no matter what we name them.

A lamp made from a tuna can does not come with a CYA (Cover Your Fanny) disclaimer or legalistic safety warnings. Is such a lamp safe? Safe *enough* for you to use? Only you can decide that. But please take note. Nowhere do I claim that a tuna fish can is idiot-proof.

Nuwick Candles

The Nuwick candle was invented in 1976 by Mary O'Brien. The Nuwick company began business in 1981. Nuwick candles were popular with Y2K preppers. They are no longer manufactured but are still available on eBay for about $10, the same as the original selling price (plus postage, of course).

Nuwick candles always reminded me of wax shoe polish in a can. Their moveable wick system was patented. You moved the wicks around with tweezers. To get additional light, more than one wick could be used at a time.

Nuwick inspired several competitors that sold multiwick candles in a can. None of them were very economical.

Taking the advertised burn times as given (and burning one wick at a time), *Coghlan's* 36-hour candle ($9) costs 25 cents per hour. *Acme* (beeswax) pencils out to 21 cents per hour.

For comparison, *Nuwick's* 120-hour candle costs 8 cents per hour. Getting the full number of hours requires running only one wick plus burning all available wax. And that means close tending of the candle and a lot of wick-moving.

Nuwick's claim of 120 hours, however, didn't sound quite right to me so I conducted a little test. Turned out there was only enough wax in the can to burn 50 hours, not 120. Point is, the hourly operating cost jumps to 19 cents per hour.

Good grief! What's wrong with a bag of tea candles from the Dollar Store? Put 'em in a baby food jar. Twenty candles for a buck; three-hour burn time per candle; 1.7¢ cents an hour.

■ **ABOVE:** *The blue Nuwick wicks are "tufted wire coils having a polyethylene and wax coating." Each wick (per the manufacturer) is good for 20 hours. To me, the wicks resemble prepped pipe cleaners twisted into the appropriate shape.* ■

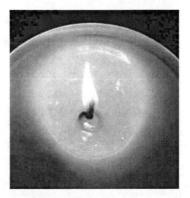

■ **ABOVE:** *To be honest, a cavern candle shielded within a tin can never struck me as the greatest light source in the world.* ■

Shoe Polish Candles

My observation that a Nuwick candle resembled a can of shoe polish triggered a couple of ideas. First, would shoe-polish wax work as candle wax? Wax is wax, right? So I melted some shoe polish in my double boiler and poured a couple of tea candles. Did it work? See below.

Pipe-Cleaner Candles

Still, why can't we make some Nuwick-style wicks out of pipe cleaners? Sounds reasonable, no? Pipe cleaners (used by smokers to clean out the goo that accumulates in their tobacco pipes) consist of a wire core covered with fuzzy cotton. If used for candles, the wire will hold the wick in place while the cotton does the wicking.

So I found some old pipe cleaners (of unknown age and unknown origin) in the shop and twisted one into the Nuwick shape. I prepped it with olive oil, drained it on a paper towel, and plunked it down on a bar of paraffin. It burned with a steady flame for several hours.

Then I tried Crisco. Took an empty tea-candle tub. Filled it with Crisco. Sat a prepped pipe-cleaner wick upon it. Lit it. Worked great.

■ **ABOVE LEFT:** *A pipe-cleaner wick (a Nuwick wannabe) setting on a bar of paraffin canning wax.* **ABOVE RIGHT:** *A pipe-cleaner wick in an old tea-candle tub filled with Crisco. Of course, if the*

flame is too high and the wick needs trimming, you'll need wire cutters. For real. ■

Encouraged by my success (with my lucky find of old pipe cleaners in the workshop), I went to Walmart to buy more. Turns out they don't sell pipe cleaners these days. Not politically correct. Even the name is not politically correct. I was directed to "Fuzzy Sticks" in the children's craft section. Fuzzy Sticks come in a wide range of colors but, unfortunately, are made from synthetic fibers that melt if lit with a match. *Fuzzy Sticks do not work as candlewicks.*

So I went on eBay. And there I found (1) regular pipe cleaners, (2) churchwarden pipe cleaners, (3) bristle pipe cleaners, (4) tapered pipe cleaners, and (5) jumbo pipe cleaners. I bought some of each, various brands.

Regular pipe cleaners are 6½" long. They are dense, of small diameter, and do not work. The Dill's brand that I remember from my own pipe-smoking days falls in this category.

Churchwarden pipe cleaners are the same as regular cleaners but are longer (12" long). They don't work.

Bristle pipe cleaners are the same as regular cleaners but have stiff plastic bristles woven in with the cotton. The plastic melts. They don't work as wicks.

Tapered pipe cleaners are big (in diameter) on one end and small (in diameter) on the other. If cut in half, the heavy end will work as a wick. Usually.

Jumbo pipe cleaners are not longer; rather, they are fluffier and bigger in diameter. Of all the styles, these are the ones that work; these are the ones you want. If you cut them in half, you'll get two Nuwick wannabes out of each pipe cleaner. BJ Long (brand) jumbos cost 7-8 cents each on eBay including postage. Whatever brand and style you try, just be sure they are cotton, not synthetic.

■ **ABOVE:** *With the BJ Long brand, the "jumbo" package is labeled exactly the same as the regular size. It's just that there are 60 jumbos in a package instead of 100. Buyer beware.* ■

Gouda Cheese-Wax Candles

Mr. Hax of crayon-candle fame also touted emergency candles made from Gouda-cheese wax. So it was with some trepidation that I journeyed down the cheese aisle of the local supermarket. Turned out I was pleasantly surprised.

■ **ABOVE:** *A 7-ounce Gouda cheese wheel. The cheese is coated with red wax with a cellophane wrapper over that. It's the wax that we're interested in.* ■

■ **ABOVE:** *Here's a circle of wax cut from one side of the wheel. I trimmed it square and rolled it up into a candle with a prepped wick in the center. (At room temperature the wax was too brittle to roll tightly without cracking so I cheated and used a hair dryer.)* ■

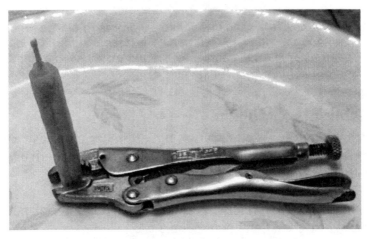

■ **ABOVE:** *The candle was 3" high. Visegrips made a good candlestick.* ■

■ **ABOVE:** *Here's the Gouda-cheese-wax candle in operation. The dripping illustrates why tea candles are superior to taper-style candles when it comes to utilizing available fuel. In a tea candle, the wax cannot escape. Though it melts, it is trapped and must feed the flame. This candle weighed 10 grams to start, burned 25 minutes, and the drippings left behind weighed 5 grams. Had this wax been used in a tea candle, everything would have burned and nothing would have been left behind.* ■

Rushlights & Mullein

Rushlights deserve explanation but are more a curiosity than a practical means of illumination. Then again, perhaps my generation is just not desperate enough.

Rushlights were widely used in Merry Olde England but carried a stigma. Only poor people used them.

To make rushlights, we first of all require the correct rush, a weedy plant that grows near streams and in marshy places. In England, that was *Juncus effusus*, the soft rush. The books say it is also found in North America.

So we gather the mature rush stalks in late summer and soak them underwater; if they dry out they are useless.

They must be peeled because it's the pith in the center of the stalk that soaks up the greasy fuel. But not all of the outer layer or rind can be peeled off. If it is, the inner pith will be limp, like a piece of string. So a thin end-to-end strip of "bark" must remain on the rush as support for the pith. Rush-peeling is not for amateurs; it's a job for a skilled and well-practiced thumbnail.

The peeled rushes (each with its lengthwise strip of bark) are dried. They range from 12 to 28 inches in length. After drying, they're soaked in household grease, bacon fat, or mutton fat. The small ones burn for ten minutes; the big ones, nearly an hour. Fifteen or twenty minutes is average.

They're clipped in a holder and burned at a 45-degree angle (or whatever angle works best for the reed at hand). While burning, they're tricky to control. They smoke. They drip on the floor. With their short burn times and fickle nature they need constant tending, a job for the children. Mother, busy with her needlework, doesn't want to get her fingers greasy.

To be honest, rushlights puzzle me. The simple vegetable-oil lamp design given earlier would be just as thrifty (or so it seems to me) with any available fuel plus give steadier light plus be a lot less messy.

While on this *au naturel* theme, I should mention mullein (*Verbascum thapsus*). It was once called the "candlewick plant." Before cotton was available, dried, folded mullein leaves were used as candlewicks. Mullein is a tall plant with yellow flowers, found in pastures and along roadsides. The plant, a single stalk, is up to 6' tall (taller than either foxglove or lupine which it resembles); the leaves up to 15" long.

Mullein originally native to Europe, is now common in the U.S.

Canning-Wax Candles

Candles can be made from bars of canning wax. Doing so is super-simple. (Unfortunately, I've long since lost track of where I can across this idea and so cannot give proper credit.)

■ **ABOVE:** *"Canning wax" is paraffin (at least in the USA). When Americans say "paraffin" they mean solid wax as shown here. When the British say "paraffin" they mean liquid kerosene.* ■

■ **ABOVE:** *The first step is to split a bar of canning wax into thirds (lengthwise). The easiest way I've found is to heavily score the bar with a utility knife, then clamp the wax in a vise and give it a sharp sideways rap with a mallet. Use a short piece of board between the mallet and the wax to spread out the blow. You want the wax to break along the score line. A second method is to use a hacksaw. That, too, works well.* ■

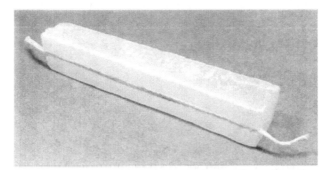

■ **ABOVE:** *The wick needs to be prepped but you don't have to sauté it in liquid wax as we did earlier for the tea candles. You can just seesaw the wick back and forth over the end of a paraffin bar or over the end of another candle or soak it in cooking oil or rub butter into it. After the wick is prepped, score one of the paraffin sticks lengthwise with a knife blade (or hacksaw) and press the wick into the groove. Use your fingers or a screwdriver blade to force the wick into the crack, whatever works. It's not a fussy big deal.* ■

■ **ABOVE:** *It is extremely unsafe to put the wax directly on the stove burner; it will likely start a fire. So here we have a saucepan with water in it setting on the stove burner. And atop the saucepan we have a frying pan (or griddle) with a flat bottom. Steam from the saucepan will heat the griddle and melt the wax.* ■

■ **ABOVE:** *Griddle FLATNESS is important because we don't want to introduce a curve in the silhouettes of our paraffin sticks. As soon as the wax starts to melt (and it only takes a couple of seconds) press the sticks together wet-face to wet-face. Don't linger. We're not looking to melt wax; we just want to glue the sticks together.* ■

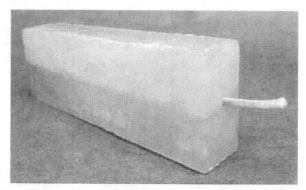

■ **ABOVE:** *Done. This one came out pretty good with a smooth seam and no gaps. But even if gaps do exist the candle will operate just fine. Heat from the candle flame melts a bit of wax, forming a pool. The liquid pool heals the gaps as well as feeding*

the flame. As the candle burns, gaps simply close up and disappear along the way. ∎

∎ **ABOVE:** *With my jackknife, I whittled the butt end of this candle to fit the candlestick. But I also heated the candlestick and custom melt-fitted (to coin a phrase) the candle to the hole that would receive it.* ∎

Safety

Let's end this booklet as we began, with safety. From the American Red Cross: "**Use only flashlights** for emergency lighting. Never use candles due to extreme risk of fire!" [emphasis theirs] —

http://www.nyredcross.org/?nd=blackout_safety_guide

Oh golly gosh gee whiz. I wonder where birthday cakes fit in. And, oh, eeek! Just think about Jack-O-Lanterns! And churches! Think about churches and candlelight services with untrained amateurs holding frightening, hazardous, perilous candles. And that 1989 Leipzig march that brought down the Berlin Wall. OMG. 70,000 men holding candles. How unsafe was that?

Can you imagine? *CANDLES!*

Good Lord, folks. Get a grip.

• "But I followed the Red Cross recommendation. I was an obedient citizen and didn't light any candles. And that kept me safe. Even when I tripped in the dark and fell down the stairs. I was safe for the whole night, right there in the stairwell, until they found me."

• Let's say that you, dear reader, do something exceptionally stupid and start a fire. What are you likely to tell the fire department? The truth? And the insurance company? The truth? Or will you fib and blame it on a candle? That lie becomes part of the database analyzed by Red Cross statisticians. Ever hear of GIGO (garbage in, garbage out)?

I once shared a taxi ride with a bunch of overpriced consultants traveling from the hotel to the job site. The cabbie had a fender-bender. Nobody was hurt. We – lined up on the sidewalk in our suits and ties and briefcases and looking at our wristwatches – all told the investigating officer that we were wearing seatbelts. And guess what. We all lied. And guess what. Our lies became part of the database.

• Could it be that Energizer is a bigger contributor to the Red Cross than Yankee Candle? Or that Red Cross objectivity has been skewed by Duracell lobbyists?

Lobbyists? Shades of Casablanca! I am shocked.

Afterword
Much of the material in this booklet comes from Chapter Two of *Lanterns, Lamps & Candles*, a book-length CD in PDF format from **www.rc-publishing.com**.

Shortly after publication I queried readers: "You recently purchased *Lanterns, Lamps & Candles*. Was it money well spent? Would you recommend it to friends? How does it rate on a scale of 1 to 10?" I received some very positive feedback:

• *YES. A steal at that price. YES – and I have recommended it and if you need to use me as a reference please do so.*

*Honestly, it's a 10+. Nothing else comes close. LOVED it. –
J.S., Oregon*

My other offerings on the lighting theme include (1) a
YouTube demo entitled *Converting a Gas Lantern to
Kerosene* and (2) *The Amazing 2000-Hour Flashlight*
(available from Amazon in both paperback and Kindle
format).

The YouTube video generated this response:

• *Ron, this is one of the best and most professional videos on
YouTube. Your organization, detail, stage presence, and
voice are fantastic.* — Guiding Mike

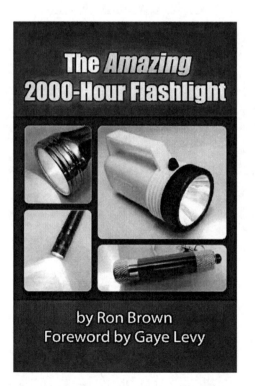

And the flashlight book received flattering reviews as well:

- *Perfect. Short, sweet, and to the point with clear, concise instructions. And infinitely readable. I was educated and entertained. It was worth every penny and then some.* — Amazon Customer

- *Well written. Informative. Easily understood. Gives sources and part numbers. Can't ask for better.* — LucMee

- *I will be looking for more books from this author.* — Charles Donaghe

Hey, this is great! Now, whenever I get down on myself because some editor has rejected me and refused to publish my stuff, I can console myself with reader evaluations. Silly editors.

CPSIA information can be obtained at www.ICGtesting.com
Printed in the USA
LVOW12s1504200515

439231LV00015B/740/P